Daddy, Help Me!

Written by

Ken Harvey

Illustrations by

MarySue Hermes

STRONG ARM BOOKS
Strength Wisdom Destiny

ISBN: 978-0-9830214-0-7

Strong Arm Books
An imprint of Cool River Pub, Inc.
P. O. Box 682451
Franklin, TN 37068-2451

Manufactured by Color House Graphics, Inc.,
Grand Rapids, Michigan, USA
October 2010 Job #33282

This book is for my dad who taught me the great lessons in life. Thanks DAD.

—Ken Harvey

To Loren and Ruth Hermes, with love and appreciation.

—MarySue Hermes

Daddy, Daddy,

help me be rich!

Okay, son...

now start
saving.

ROCK
SOLID

Daddy, Daddy,

help me rule the world!

Okay, I will...

now study.

THE HOBBIT
ATLAS
AMERICAN HISTORY
THE LITTLE PRINCE
CLAUDE MONET
BEAUTIFUL JOE
A CHRISTMAS CAROL
LEWIS CARROL A TANGLED TALE
NEW TESTAMENT
GULLIVER'S TRAVELS
WESTERN ART
AN AMERICAN CHILDHOOD
CHARLES DICKENS
Book of VIRTUES - BENNETT -
O HENRY
QUIET STRENGTH
MOZART
WINNIE THE POOH
WHEN CHOCOLATE MILK MOVED IN
LORD OF THE RINGS
MICHNER
AND the GLORY

Daddy, Daddy,

help me
be strong!

1st
PLACE

Okay, son...

push one
more time!

COLD'S GYM

Daddy, Daddy,

help me to fly!

Okay, son...

now fly!

Daddy, Daddy,

teach me to fight!

Okay, son...

I'll teach you what's worth fighting for.

Daddy, Daddy,

help me
grow tall!

Okay, son...

is this
tall enough?

Daddy, Daddy,

why do you
help me so much?

I help you son...

because I love you,
and so that
one day
you may
help others.

Draw a line connecting each circle picture to its matching square picture.